MY SWEET KITCHEN

ADARSH KUMAWAT

ISBN 979-888555296-7

I dedicate this book

to

My loving Parents, Rakesh Kumawat & Jolly Kumawat

My dear Lavisha,

Thank you for being the guiding light when life threw me in the darkest
of corners

You are the sun in my day, the wind in my sky, the waves in my ocean,
and the beat in my heart.

Contents

Contents

CHAPTER ONE

KAJU KATLI

INGREDIENTS

- 1 cup cashews – 160 grams
- ½ cup sugar – 100 grams sugar
- 5 tablespoons water
- 1 tablespoon Ghee or coconut oil or any neutral tasting oil (optional)
- 1 teaspoon chopped rose petals or 1 teaspoon rose water or 8 to 9 strands of saffron (optional)

INSTRUCTION
Grinding Cashews

- Powder the cashew in a coffee grinder, blender or a dry grinder.
- The cashews should be in powdered form and not become pasty or oily.

Making Dough

- On a low flame heat sugar and water in a thick bottomed or non stick pan or kadai.
- Meanwhile grease a plate or a tray and keep aside or keep butter papers ready.
- When all the sugar has dissolved in the water, add the cashew powder. There is no consistency in the sugar syrup required like one string or two string. Just let the sugar dissolve in the water and then proceed with the next step.
- Mix and keep on stirring the cashew mixture non-stop on a low flame.
- The cashew mixture would start thickening.

- Cook the kaju mixture for approx 7 to 9 minutes until the whole dough starts to come together.

Kneading

- Remove the whole lump of the kaju dough from the pan and place it on your work surface or in a bowl or plate.
- Add the rose petals and ghee or oil to the cashew mixture.
- When the heat in the dough is hot enough to handle, then knead the cashew mixture lightly.
- Flatten the dough and place it on a butter paper or on a greased plate or tray.
- Place a butter paper on top and then using a rolling pin, roll gently the dough from all sides till you reach a thickness of 3 to 5 mm in the dough.
- Remove the butter paper and let the rolled dough cool.
- When completely cooled, using a sharp knife cut the cashew dough giving square or diamond shapes.
- Gently remove the kaju katli with a butter knife.
- Serve the kaju katli straight away or keep in an airtight container.

CHAPTER TWO

RASGULLA

INGREDIENTS

- 1 litre full fat whole cow's milk
- 2 to 3 tablespoon lemon juice, add as required
- 2 cups sugar
- 4 cups water or 1 litre water
- 1 tablespoon milk (optional)
- 1 teaspoon sooji (rava or cream of wheat) or all purpose flour or corn starch
- 1 to 2 tablespoon rose water or kewra water or ½ teaspoon cardamom powder

INSTRUCTION
Making Chenna

- Take milk in a pan and keep it to boil on a low to medium flame.
- When the milk comes to a boil, then reduce the flame to its lowest. Add 1 to 3 tbsp lemon juice. First add 1 tbsp lemon juice and stir. If the milk has not curdled completely, then add 1 tbsp more. Keep the lemon juice handy with you.
- As soon as the milk curdles, switch off the flame. The milk should curdle completely with the green watery whey. If the milk does not curdle, then add ½ to 1 tbsp of lemon juice more.
- Now pour the curdled milk in the cheese cloth/muslin lined strainer or bowl.
- Now squeeze the muslin with your hands very well, so that excess water is drained from the chenna. Remember there should not be excess water

or moisture in the chenna as then the rasgulla will break when cooking.

- Place a heavy weight on the chenna for 7 to 8 minutes. You can also hang the chenna for about 30 minutes.

Making Rasgulla Balls

- After 7 to 8 minutes, remove the cheesecloth from the chenna. Note that the chenna should not have too much moisture nor be too dry.
- Add 1 tsp sooji or rava or semolina. You can also add all purpose flour (maida). Adding either of them helps to bind the mixture. For a gluten free option, add corn starch instead of semolina or all purpose flour.
- First mix the sooji with chenna and then begin to knead.
- With the heels of your palms mash the chenna and knead. Keep on collecting the chenna from the sides and continue to mash and knead.

This kneading process is very important and also decides the texture of chenna. When you feel your palms becoming a bit greasy, its time to stop. Just a bit of greasiness is required.

Avoid kneading to an extent where the whole chenna becomes greasy. I kneaded for about 10 minutes as I have very light hands. So depending on the quality of chenna and the pressure you apply while kneading, you can take more or less time. Note that the chenna should just begin to get greasy.

- Knead to a smooth ball of chenna.
- Now pinch small portions from the chenna and roll them between your palms to a smooth round ball.
- Prepare all small balls this way. Cover all the chenna balls with a moist muslin or kitchen towel and keep aside.

Making Sugar Syrup For Rasgulla

- In a large pan, take 2 cups sugar and 4 cups water.
- Add 1 tbsp milk and stir. Adding milk helps in removing impurities. If there are no impurities then you don't need to add milk and directly proceed to step 6
- Once the sugar solution becomes hot, the impurities begin to float on the top. You can either remove it with a spoon. Or strain the impurities in a cheese cloth/muslin lined strainer.

Now from the purified sugar solution, reserve ½ cup in a cup or mug. This ½ cup of sugar solution we will be adding to the cooking rasgulla.

Reserve another 1 cup of the sugar solution in a serving bowl.

Cooking Rasgulla

- The rest of the 2.5 cups of sugar solution you add it back to the large pan and bring it to a boil on a medium high flame.
- Slid the rasgulla gently into the sugar solution.
- Once all the rasgulla have been added to the sugar solution, shake the pan. Don't stir the rasgulla with a spoon. Just gently shake the pan.

Cover immediately with a lid and let them cook. Keep the flame to a medium or medium high.

- After 4 minutes, open the lid and add ¼ cup of the reserved sugar solution. Shake the pan. Adding this reserved sugar solution ensures that the temperature & consistency of the sugar solution is maintained and the sugar does not cook to its thread consistencies.

Cover again and continue to cook.

- After 4 minutes, again add ¼ cup of the reserved sugar solution. Cover and again cook for 2 minutes. I cooked for 10 minutes. The timing will vary depending on the thickness & quality of pan, the depth of the pan and flame intensity.

To Check The Doneness Of Rasgulla

- There are two ways. First place the rasgulla in a bowl or cup of water. If the rasgulla sinks to the bottom its cooked.
- Second method is to press a small portion of the rasgulla with your finger. If the pressed portion bounces back to its original shape, its cooked
- Once they are cooked, switch off the flame and keep the pan down.

Serving The Rasgulla

- Now take each rasgulla with a spoon and place it in the bowl containing the 1 cup of sugar solution. Cover and keep aside.
- Let the sugar solution in which the rasgulla were cooked, become warm. Then add this to the serving bowl containing the rasgulla.
- Once the whole mixture has cooled down, add 1 to 2 tbsp rose water.
- If you don't have rose water you can also kewra water (pandanus extract) or ½ tsp cardamom powder. Stir gently and allow them to be soaked in the sugar syrup for 30 minutes.

You can serve the rasgulla now or refrigerate them and serve later.

CHAPTER THREE

ALWAR KA MAWA

INGREDIENTS

- 6 cups Whole Milk
- 3 tbsp Lemon Juice
- ½ cup Sugar
- ⅛ tsp Crushed Cardamom
- 2 tbsp Ghee or unsalted butter
- 1 tbsp Pistachios for garnish

INSTRUCTION

- Preheat oven to 350 degrees, gas mark 4. Grease a 6-inch plate and set aside.
- In a large saucepan bring the milk to a boil over medium- high heat, letting it boil for 2-3 minutes.
- Into the milk, add the lemon juice and it will begin to curdle – boil for 5 minutes. Remove 1 ½ cups of the whey (liquid remaining after milk has been curdled).
- Continue to cook and stir occasionally until the milk is a grainy consistency and the whey has evaporated – cook for 15-20 minutes.
- Add in the sugar and cardamom, keep stirring until the mixture thickens – about 5 minutes.
- Transfer mixture to the greased pan sprinkle sliced pistachios on top. Cook for 5-10 minutes until golden brown on top.
- Let the cake sit for an hour before slicing.

CHAPTER FOUR

GULAB JAMUN

INGREDIENTS
for Jamun:

- 1.5 cup (100 grams) milk powder, unsweetened
- 1 cup (60 grams) maida / plain flour
- 1 tsp baking powder
- 4 tbsp ghee / clarified butter
- milk (for kneading)
- ghee or oil (for frying)

for Sugar syrup:

- 4 cup sugar
- 4 cup water
- 4 cardamom
- 0.5 tsp saffron / kesar
- 2 tsp lemon juice
- 2 tsp rose water

INSTRUCTION

- firstly, in a large bowl take ¾ cup milk powder, ½ cup maida and ½ tsp baking powder.
- mix well, homemade gulab jamun mix is ready.
- now add 2 tbsp ghee and mix well making the flour moist.
- further, add milk as required start to combine.
- combine well forming a soft dough. do not knead the dough.

- cover and rest for 10 minutes.
- meanwhile, prepare the sugar syrup by taking 2 cup sugar, 2 cup water, 2 cardamom and ¼ tsp saffron.
- mix well and boil for 5 minutes or until the sugar syrup turns sticky. do not attain any string consistency.
- turn off the flame and add 1 tsp lemon juice and 1 tsp rose water. lemon juice is added to prevent sugar syrup from crystallizing.
- cover and keep the sugar syrup aside.
- after 10 minutes or resting the dough, start to prepare small ball sized jamuns.
- make sure there are no cracks in the jamun. if there are cracks then there are high chances for jamuns to break while frying.
- deep fry in medium hot oil or ghee. frying in ghee gives good flavour to jamuns.
- stir continuously and fry on low flame.
- fry until the jamuns turn golden brown.
- drain off and transfer the jamun into a hot sugar syrup.
- cover and rest for 2 hours or until jamuns absorb the sugar syrup and doubles in size.
- finally, enjoy gulab jamun with ice cream or as it is.

CHAPTER FIVE

RASMALAI

INGREDIENTS
For the rasmalai balls

- 1 liter whole milk
- 4 tablespoons lemon juice
- 1 teaspoon cornflour
- 4 cups water
- 1 cup sugar

For the ras [syrup]

- 500 ml whole milk
- 5-6 green cardamom pods peeled and crushed to get the powder
- saffron a pinch
- 3-4 tablespoons sugar
- finely chopped pistachios

INSTRUCTION
Rasmalai Balls

- Boil milk in a heavy bottom pan.Once it comes to a boil, switch off the flame and add 1/2 cup of water to bring the temperature of the milk down a bit.
- Wait for 5-10 minutes and then start adding lemon juice till milk curdles.
- Add lemon juice till the milk curdles completely.
- Using a strainer drain the water and collect the chena.
- Rinse it under tap water so that there's no trace of lemon juice in it.

- Leave it in the strainer for 10-15 minutes and then take the chena in your hand and squeeze out remaining water slowly.
- Add cornflour and start mashing the chena till it's smooth.
- Set the clock to 10 minutes and mash constantly for 10 minutes using your palm. Once it's smooth, make small balls out of it.
- Heat 1 cup sugar and 4 cups water in a wide pan and wait till it comes to a full boil.
- Drop the balls in boiling sugar syrup and cook for 15-17 minutes. The balls will double in size by then.
- Take out the balls from the syrup and drop them in fresh water. If they sink to the bottom, the balls are done.

Thickened Milk

- In a heavy bottom pan, boil 500 ml of milk.
- Soak few strands of saffron in a tablespoon of warm milk and set aside.
- Once the milk comes to a boil, lower the flame and continue to stir the milk at regular intervals. After 10 minutes add sugar and mix.
- After 20-25 minutes the milk will thicken to desired consistency, add soaked saffron and crushed cardamom.
- Also add finely chopped pistachios [if using]. Mix and switch off the flame.
- Take out the cooled rasmalai balls from the sugar syrup, squeeze and flatten with your hands.
- Transfer the balls to thickened milk [milk should be warm].
- Chill in the refrigerator overnight or for 5-6 hours. Garnish with chopped pistachios and few saffron strands before serving.

CHAPTER SIX

RAJBHOG

INGREDIENTS

for paneer balls:

- 1½ litre milk (cow)
- 2 tbsp lemon juice
- 1 tbsp rava / semolina / suji
- pinch saffron food colour
- pinch cardamom powder
- 2 tbsp crushed dry fruits (cashew, pistachios, almonds)

for sugar syrup:

- 1½ cup sugar
- 8 cup water
- 2 tbsp saffron / kesar water

INSTRUCTION

- firstly, knead fresh paneer till it turns out smooth texture without any grains of milk.
- now add a tbsp of suji, pinch saffron food colour and pinch cardamom powder.
- knead further for 5 more minutes or until a soft dough is formed.
- pinch a small ball sized ball and flatten it.
- place ½ tsp crushed dry fruit in the centre.
- get the edges together, and make a round ball without any cracks. keep aside.

- sugar syrup recipe:
- firstly, in a deep vessel take 1½ cup of sugar.
- furthermore, add 8 cups of water and 2 tbsp saffron.
- boil the syrup for 10 minutes on medium flame.
- after that, drop the prepared paneer balls into boiling sugar syrup.
- cover and boil for 15 minutes. the paneer balls will have doubled in size.
- furthermore, keep aside till it cools completely and then refrigerate.
- finally, serve rajbhog / kesar rasgulla chilled or at room temperature garnished with few saffron strands.

CHAPTER SEVEN

MOONG DAL HALWA

INGREDIENTS

- 1 cup moong dal (spilt husked yellow mung lentils)
- 9 to 10 tablespoon Ghee (clarified butter)
- 4 green cardamoms, husked and powdered in a mortar-pestle or ¼ to ⅓ teaspoon cardamom powder
- 10 to 12 unsalted pistachios - sliced or chopped or 10 to 12 blanched almonds - sliced
- 1 tablespoon golden raisins
- 1 cup full fat whole milk
- 2 cups water
- 1 or 1.25 cups regular sugar or organic unrefined cane sugar

INSTRUCTION

- Soak the moong dal or mung lentils, in enough water overnight or for 4 to 5 hours.
- Drain and then grind the moong dal to a smooth paste with 1/4 or 1/3 cup water.
- Melt ghee in a non stick pan. Add the ground moong dal. Stir well
- Keep on stirring the halwa on a low to medium flame. The halwa has the raw aroma of the moong lentils and it should go away completely before you start with the next step. So till then you have to stir and cook the halwa.
- The halwa first is pasty, then starts getting lumpy and then starts breaking down and getting separated with the fat releasing from the sides. Break the lumps while stirring.

- Meanwhile when the halwa is cooking, in another pan or kadai, take milk, water and sugar. Keep this pan on the stove top and stir so that the sugar dissolves. On a low or medium flame, heat this milk-water-sugar mixture till it comes to a boil.
- The moong dal mixture should reach a granular consistency before you add the hot milk mixture. You should get a fried aroma from the mung lentils and the color should become a light golden. The fat also should get separated.
- When the milk mixture comes to a boil, add it to the fried mung lentils.
- The mixture sizzles, so be careful while adding the hot milk and water mixture.
- Stir well. Simmer and cook stirring often.
- The liquid should get absorbed and once again you will see the ghee getting separated.
- Lastly add cardamom powder, chopped pistachios and raisins.
- Serve moong dal ka halwa hot. You can also garnish with some pistachios and serve.

CHAPTER EIGHT

RABRI MALPUA

INGREDIENTS

For malpua

- Plain Flour 1 cup (maida)
- Mawa 1/2 cup (unsweetened khoya) a little less than half cup will also do
- Saunf powder 1/4 tsp (optional)
- Cardamom powder 1/2 tsp
- Salt pinch
- Sugar 1 tbsp
- Milk 2 cups
- Ghee 1/2 cup for frying (you can use oil also)
- Pistachios fistful, sliced
- Almonds 8-10, blanched, peeled and slivered
- Saffron 7-8 strands

For sugar syrup:

- Sugar 3/4 cup
- Water 1/3 cup
- Cardamom powder 1/4 tsp
- Saffron 4 strands

INSTRUCTION

- Bring the milk to a boil and simmer till it reduces to 1 1/2 cups. Turn off flame and allow to cool to luke warm temperature.

- In a bowl, add khoya and half of the boiled milk and mix till it is smooth. Add cardamom powder, saunf powder, sugar, salt and few strands of saffron and mix well. Add half of the flour and mix well till there are no lumps.
- Add the remaining flour and mix well. Slowly add the milk till it forms a smooth flowing batter as shown in the picture above. Keep mixing the mixture for 3-4 mts and set aside till you make the sugar syrup.
- To prepare sugar syrup, add sugar and water in a stainless steel vessel and allow the sugar to melt . Simmer the sugar syrup for 10-12 mts on low medium flame. Add cardamom powder and turn off heat. Set aside.
- Heat ghee in a small vessel or pan on low medium flame for 3-4 mts. Pour a small ladle full of batter in the center of the pan without spreading it. The batter will spread on its own. Do not try to touch the pancake till it starts to turn golden along the edges. It will slowly get immersed in the ghee and cook on medium flame till the sides are golden brown.
- Flip it over and cook on medium flame for another 2-3 mts or till it turns golden brown. Use a slotted spoon to drain the Malpua and place it in the sugar syrup immediately. Fully immerse the Malpua in the sugar syrup and let it sit for half a minute. Remove with a slotted spoon such that the sugar syrup drains off the Malpua and then place it on a serving plate.
- At the time of serving, place malpua on a serving plate. Spoon some rabri on top of the malpua and garnish with chopped pistachios and almond slivers.

CHAPTER NINE

SHAHI TUKDA

INGREDIENTS

- 6 slices White bread slices
- Ghee for frying
- ¾ + ¼ cup Sugar
- 1 cup Water
- 2-3 pods Cardamom (crushed)
- 1 litre Full cream milk
- 15-20 strands Saffron
- ½ tsp Rose Water
- Slivers of almonds and pistachios to garnish

INSTRUCTION

- Cut the corners of bread slices and cut the slices diagonally.
- Heat the ghee and when it is hot, deep fry the bread slices till golden brown.
- Remove on a tissue lined plate.
- Heat water in a pan and add ½ cup of sugar to it.
- Add cardamom to the water.
- Let it boil for 6-8 minutes.
- Remove the pan from heat and keep aside.
- Heat milk in a heavy bottom pan.
- When it comes to a boil, add saffron and rose water and reduce the heat and let it simmer till it reduce to half.
- Keep stirring in between.
- Add sugar and thicken it a little more.

- Dip bread slices in sugar syrup for 5-10 seconds. (or more if you like softer version)
- Keep them on the serving plate.
- Top with the reduced milk.
- Garnish with almonds and pistachios slivers.
- Serve immediately.

CHAPTER TEN

DOODH PEDA

INGREDIENTS

- 200 to 205 grams grated khoya or 1 cup tightly packed grated khoya (mawa or evaporated and dried milk solids)
- ½ cup sugar or 125 grams sugar, add as required
- ½ teaspoon cardamom powder
- 2 to 3 tablespoons milk
- 3 to 4 pistachios or almonds , thinly sliced

INSTRUCTION

- First grate or crumble 200 to 205 grams of khoya. Take the grated khoya in a heavy kadai or pan. You will need 1 cup tightly packed grated khoya. You can use homemade or store brought khoya. I have used instant khoya.
- Add ½ cup sugar (125 grams) and ½ teaspoon cardamom powder.
- Keep the pan on a stove top on a low flame.
- Then mix the khoya with the sugar very well.
- Next add 2 to 3 tablespoons milk. mix well.
- You will see the sugar melting and the mixture getting a liquid consistency.
- Continuously keep on stirring and simmer the peda mixture. You have to stir non-stop so that the mixture does not get browned from the bottom.
- Stir often and the mixture will start bubbling.
- Continue to stir and cook till the mixture thickens and leaves the sides of the pan.

- Then immediately pour the entire peda mixture in a steel plate or a tray. When you pour the mixture it will still be in a molten state but thickened. Do not over cook as then the pedas will become chewy.
- Let it become warm at room temperature.

Making Doodh Peda

- Now take small portions from the lukewarm peda mixture and roll them in small to medium balls.
- Place a few slivered pistachios or almonds on top of each peda ball.
- With a peda maker, press each ball to give a distinct design on top of it. If you do not have a peda maker, then just roll the mixture in balls and then flatten them. Press a few almonds or pistachios on top.
- Make a design on all doodh peda with the peda maker. In case the doodh peda fall flat and do not hold shape, then they are slightly undercooked. Gather all the mixture together and heat again in the pan for 2 to 3 minutes or till the mixture leaves sides of the pan.
- Now you can store the milk peda for a few hours at room temperature and then serve later. Leftovers can be refrigerated. This doodh peda recipe yields 12 medium sized pedas.

CHAPTER ELEVEN

GHEVAR

INGREDIENTS

For batter

- ½ cup ghee / clarified butter
- 1 block ice
- 2 cup maida / plain flour / refined flour
- ½ cup milk, chilled
- 3 cup water, chilled
- 1 tsp lemon juice

For sugar syrup

- 1 cup sugar
- ¼ cup water

Other ingredients

- oil / ghee for deep frying
- dry fruits, for garnishing
- ¼ tsp cardamom powder / elachi powder
- silver vrak for garnishing

INSTRUCTION

- firstly, take ½ cup ghee and rub with ice block.
- now add 2 cup maida and crumble well.
- further, add ½ cup chilled milk and give a rough mix.

- additionally, add 3 cup of chilled water, 1 tsp lemon juice and make a smooth flowing consistency
- pour the 2 tbsp of batter keeping a good distance from hot oil.
- the batter will splatter and later the froth subsides. repeat 10-15 times
- pull the ghevar out once cooked, and drain off the oil completely.
- pour the sugar syrup over ghevar, garnish with chopped nuts and sprinkle cardamom powder.
- finally, garnish the ghevar with silver vrak or rabri and ready to serve.

CHAPTER TWELVE

CHOCOLATE BARFI

INGREDIENTS

- 700 grams khoya / mawa (grated)
- 1 cup (225 grams) sugar
- 2 tbsp cocoa powder

INSTRUCTION

- firstly, in a large kadai take 700 grams khoya. make sure to grate it or crumble the khoya for uniform cooking.
- add 1 cup ((225 grams)) sugar and start to mix.
- keeping the flame on low, continuously stir until the khova and sugar melt.
- mash the khova making sure there are no lumps.
- cook until the mixture thickens and starts to separate from the pan. takes approximately 10 minutes.
- divide the mixture into 2 equal parts. and transfer 1 half of the mixture to the tray lined with baking paper.
- press and level up uniformly. i have used the tray of size: 6 inch x 3 inch.
- to the remaining half of the mixture, add 2 tbsp cocoa powder and mix well.
- continue to cook until everything is well combined.
- transfer the mixture over the burfi layer forming double-decker layer.
- press and level up uniformly.
- now rest for 30 minutes or until the burfi sets.
- finally, cut into pieces and enjoy chocolate burfi.

CHAPTER THIRTEEN

KESAR PISTA KULFI

INGREDIENTS

- 1.5 litre milk (full cream)
- ¼ cup cream (optional)
- ¼ cup sugar (adjust to your sweetness)
- 20 pistachios (chopped)
- 2 tbsp saffron milk
- ½ tsp cardamom powder

INSTRUCTION

- firstly, in a thick bottomed pan take 1.5 - 2 litres of full cream milk and get to a boil.
- once the milk comes to a boil, add cream and give a good stir.
- furthermore, simmer for 30 minutes and keep stirring in between.
- next, add sugar and give a good mix.
- simmer for 5 minutes or till the milk thickens completely.
- additionally, add chopped pistachios, saffron milk and cardamom powder.
- then give a mix and simmer further more for 5 minutes.
- allow the thickened milk to cool completely. this may take atleast an hour.
- after the milk is cooled completely, transfer them to kulfi moulds or to a plastic glass.
- cover the glass with cling wrap or you can use aluminium foil.
- furthermore, freeze the cup for atleast 5 hours or overnight.

- after 5 hours or more when the kufi is set completely. insert a stick in between the cup.
- then slowly warm up by rubbing in between your hands. you can also dip in warm water.
- gently, remove the kulfi from the glass / mould and garnish with few chopped pistachios.
- finally, serve kulfi immediately.

CHAPTER FOURTEEN

PHIRNI

INGREDIENTS

- 3 tablespoons Basmati rice
- ¼ cup Water
- 5 Almonds blanched, peeled & sliced
- 5 Pistachios blanched & sliced
- 4 cups or 1 liter Milk
- ⅓ cup Sugar
- ¼ teaspoon Green cardamom seeds powder
- 3-4 strands Saffron
- 1 teaspoon Rose water

INSTRUCTION

- Blanch the almonds and pistachios by soaking in boiling hot water for 20-30 minutes. After that peel the skin and slice them.
- Also, wash the rice and soak for 20 minutes.
- After that discard the soaking water and grind into coarse paste using fresh ¼ cup of water.
- Take milk into heavy bottom pan and bring it to a boil on medium heat.
- Once starts boiling add coarsely ground rice and cook for 15-28 minutes or till the rice is cooked and milk is thickened. Do stir in between and scrap the pan, so milk does not stick and burn.
- Then add sugar, cardamom powder and saffron. Mix well and cook for 5 minutes.
- Now add rose water and turn off the stove.

- Pour into individual serving bowls, garnish with sliced almonds, pistachios and crushed saffron strands.
- Cover it and chill in refrigerator for few hours and then serve.

28

CHAPTER FIFTEEN

CHENNA TOAST

INGREDIENTS

- 5,6 servings
- 1/2 liter Milk
- 1 cup Yogurt
- Pinch light brown colour
- 1 tbsp Corn flour
- 2 cups Sugar
- 2 cups Milk
- as needed Saffron

INSTRUCTION

- Milk in a deep pan and bring to a boil.
- Once the milk starts boiling. Add curd slowly and keep stirring. Allow it to stand for 1/2 minute to curdle.
- Make sure you keep stirring on a slow flame till completely curdled when the chenna and the water separates out..
- Strain using a muslin cloth.place the muslin cloth with the chenna in a bowl of fresh water and wash it.
- The process of straining and washing chenna sTie and hang for 4o to 50mins for the extra water to drain out. Make sure there is no water in chenna else the rasgullas will break.
- Place the muslin cloth on a flat plate open it and knead the chenna with cornflour and mix well.
- Using your palms for 3-4 mins or till the chenna is smooth and free of lumps.

- It should become like dough when you knead it for some time.
- Now Put 4 cup of water in a pot add the sugar and bring to boil.
- Put the long chenna in to the sugar water and cover and steam for 7-8 min.
- Switch off the flame and allow it to stand in the steamer for 10-15 mins
- Do not touch the rasgullas when they are very hot else they might break. Remove and refrigerate for 15 mins.
- For garnishing - Boil milk in a pan till it is reduced to half and becoms thick and creamy.
- Add half of coconut powder. Add sugar and keep aside to cool.
- Once it's cool down garnish your chenna toast with 1 tbsp of this mixture.
- Garnish with saffron and dry fruits optional.

CHAPTER SIXTEEN

CARROT CAKE

INGREDIENTS
Cake:

- 4 eggs
- 1 ¼ cups vegetable oil
- 2 cups white sugar
- 2 teaspoons vanilla extract
- 2 cups all-purpose flour
- 2 teaspoons baking soda
- 2 teaspoons baking powder
- ½ teaspoon salt
- 2 teaspoons ground cinnamon
- 3 cups grated carrots
- 1 cup chopped pecans

Frosting:

- ½ cup butter, softened
- 8 ounces cream cheese, softened
- 4 cups confectioners' sugar
- 1 teaspoon vanilla extract
- 1 cup chopped pecans

INSTRUCTION

- Preheat oven to 350 degrees F (175 degrees C). Grease and flour a 9x13 inch pan.

- In a large bowl, beat together eggs, oil, white sugar and 2 teaspoons vanilla. Mix in flour, baking soda, baking powder, salt and cinnamon. Stir in carrots. Fold in pecans. Pour into prepared pan.
- Bake in the preheated oven for 40 to 50 minutes, or until a toothpick inserted into the center of the cake comes out clean. Let cool in pan for 10 minutes, then turn out onto a wire rack and cool completely.
- To Make Frosting: In a medium bowl, combine butter, cream cheese, confectioners' sugar and 1 teaspoon vanilla. Beat until the mixture is smooth and creamy. Stir in chopped pecans.
- Frost the cooled cake.

CHAPTER SEVENTEEN

ICE CREAM

INGREDIENTS

- 1 can chilled sweetened condensed milk or 400 grams sweetened condensed milk
- 2.5 to 2.75 cups chilled whipping cream - 35% to 50% fat
- 2 teaspoons vanilla extract or 1 teaspoon vanilla essence or 1 vanilla bean or 1 teaspoon vanilla powder
- some grated chocolate for garnish - optional

INSTRUCTION

- In a large bowl, take 2.5 to 2.75 cups of chilled whipping cream (30% to 50% fat). Add 2 teaspoons vanilla extract. If using vanilla essence, then add 1 teaspoon of it.
- With an electric beater at full speed, begin to whip the cream. Timing will vary depending on the fat content in the cream. Both for amul fresh cream and amul whipping cream, it takes about 8 to 10 minutes.
- Also be careful while whipping and do not whip too much, as then the cream would get churned into butter.
- Whip till stiff peaks are formed. You can also whip till soft peaks. If using 25% fat cream, then you can whip till soft peaks.
- Now add 400 grams of chilled sweetened condensed milk (about 1.6 cups).
- Fold gently but very well. Also remember not to overfold as then the ice cream mixture can fall flat.
- Remove the vanilla ice cream mixture in a container or box and then cover it tightly. Or you can cover the same bowl (if its freezer safe) with

a tight fitting lid or aluminium foil.

- Freeze till the ice cream is set. Before serving, keep the ice cream box or bowl for some minutes at room temperature. Then using a scoop, remove the ice cream.
- Serve vanilla ice cream. You can sprinkle some chocolate chips or grated chocolate or candied fruits or even tutti frutti from top if you want.

CHAPTER EIGHTEEN

CHOCOLATE CHIP COOKIES

INGREDIENTS

- 227 g salted butter* softened
- 200 g white (granulated) sugar
- 220 g light brown sugar packed
- 2 tsp pure vanilla extract
- 2 large eggs
- 360 g all-purpose flour
- 1 tsp baking soda
- ½ tsp baking powder
- 1 tsp sea salt***
- 350 g chocolate chips (or chunks, or chopped chocolate)

INSTRUCTION

- Preheat oven to 375 degrees F. Line a baking pan with parchment paper and set aside.
- In a separate bowl mix flour, baking soda, salt, baking powder. Set aside.
- Cream together butter and sugars until combined.
- Beat in eggs and vanilla until fluffy.
- Mix in the dry ingredients until combined.
- Add 12 oz package of chocolate chips and mix well.
- Roll 2-3 TBS (depending on how large you like your cookies) of dough at a time into balls and place them evenly spaced on your prepared cookie sheets. (alternately, use a small cookie scoop to make your cookies).

- Bake in preheated oven for approximately 8-10 minutes. Take them out when they are just BARELY starting to turn brown.
- Let them sit on the baking pan for 2 minutes before removing to cooling rack

CHAPTER NINETEEN

CHOCOLATE FUDGE

INGREDIENTS

- 2 cups white sugar
- ½ cup cocoa
- 1 cup milk
- 4 tablespoons butter
- 1 teaspoon vanilla extract

INSTRUCTION

- Grease an 8x8 inch square baking pan. Set aside.
- Combine sugar, cocoa and milk in a medium saucepan. Stir to blend, then bring to a boil, stirring constantly. Reduce heat and simmer. Do not stir again.
- Place candy thermometer in pan and cook until temperature reaches 238 degrees F(114 degrees C). If you are not using a thermometer, then cook until a drop of this mixture in a cup of cold water forms a soft ball. Feel the ball with your fingers to make sure it is the right consistency. It should flatten when pressed between your fingers.
- Remove from heat. Add butter or margarine and vanilla extract. Beat with a wooden spoon until the fudge loses its sheen. Do not under beat.
- Pour into prepared pan and let cool. Cut into about 60 squares.

CHAPTER TWENTY

WALNUT BROWNIE

INGREDIENTS

- 3/4 cup all-purpose flour
- 1 cup granulated sugar
- 3/4 cup unsweetened cocoa powder
- 1/2 cup packed brown sugar
- 1/2 teaspoon baking powder
- 1/4 teaspoon salt
- 4 ounces bittersweet chocolate coarsely chopped, divided
- 1/3 cup milk
- 6 tablespoons butter
- 1 teaspoon vanilla extract
- 2 large eggs lightly beaten
- 1/2 cup chopped walnuts divided

INSTRUCTION

- Preheat oven to 350 degrees F. Coat an 8- or 9-inch square baking dish with nonstick cooking spray.
- Combine the flour, sugar, cocoa powder, brown sugar, baking powder and salt in a large mixing bowl. Set aside.
- Place half of the bittersweet chocolate and the milk in a small saucepan and place over LOW heat. Cook and stir for a minute or two and then add the butter. Continue cooking over LOW heat, stirring constantly, until the butter and chocolate have completely melted. Remove the pan from the heat and stir in the vanilla.

- Pour the melted chocolate mixture into the flour mixture in the mixing bowl and stir until slightly combined. Add the eggs, remaining bittersweet chocolate, and 1/4 cup of the walnuts (reserve remaining nuts for later) to the flour mixture; stir to combine.
- Pour the batter into prepared baking dish and sprinkle with remaining 1/4 cup walnuts.
- Bake until a wooden pick inserted in the center comes out with moist crumbs clinging, approximately 20 to 22 minutes for 9-inch baking dish or 22 to 26 minutes for a 8-inch baking dish. The edges should seem solid but the center will appear somewhat soft and will continue to set up as the brownies cool. Ovens can vary so I recommend setting your kitchen timer for a couple of minutes shy of the recommended baking times and watching them closely towards the end. Remove from the oven and cool completely in the baking dish before cutting and serving.

CHAPTER TWENTY-ONE

APPLE PIE

INGREDIENTS

- Pie dough for top and bottom 9-inch pie, chilled
- 4 to 4 1/4 pounds baking apples (7 to 8 apples)
- 1/2 cup (100 grams) light or dark brown sugar
- 1/2 cup (100 grams) granulated sugar
- 1/4 teaspoon fine sea salt
- 1 teaspoon ground cinnamon
- 1/4 teaspoon ground ginger
- 1/4 teaspoon ground cardamom
- 1/4 teaspoon ground allspice
- 1/4 teaspoon freshly grated nutmeg
- 2 tablespoons cornstarch or use 4 tablespoons tapioca flour/starch
- 1 tablespoon butter
- 1 egg

INSTRUCTION

- Peel, and then cut the apples in half. Remove the cores, and then slice apple halves into thin slices, about 1/4-inch thick. Place the apple slices into a very large bowl.
- Scatter both sugars, salt, and spices over the apples, and then use your hands to toss them, coating the apple slices as much as possible. Set aside for 1 hour at room temperature.

MAKE APPLE FILLING

- Roll out the first half of pie dough on a lightly-floured work surface. To prevent the dough from sticking and to ensure uniform thickness, roll from the center of the dough outwards and keep lifting up and turning the dough a quarter turn as you roll. Check for the correct size by inverting the pie dish over the dough. The dough should be about 1 1/2 to 2 inches larger than the dish.
- Being careful not to stretch it, place the dough into the pie dish, and then trim overhanging dough to within 3/4-inch of the edge of the dish. Refrigerate while you make the pie filling.
- Roll out the second half of dough to a similar size as before and transfer it to a large parchment-lined baking sheet. Keep this in the refrigerator until needed.

PREPARE PIE CRUST

- Position an oven rack towards the center of the oven, and then heat the oven to 400 degrees Fahrenheit (200C).

PREPARE OVEN

- Toss cornstarch (or tapioca) with the apples. Transfer most (if not all) of the apples into the prepared bottom crust, using your hands to really pack them down into the pie. Fill the pie until apples are mounded at the same height as the edge of the pie crust. If you have too many apples, save them .
- Pour the juices that have accumulated at the bottom of the bowl over the apples. (If it looks like there's more than 3/4 to 1 cup of liquid, you might want to leave some behind, see notes below). Cut a tablespoon of butter into 8 or so small pieces and dot them over the pie.
- For a double crust pie, place the second pie dough round over the filling or cut it into strips and lattice the top lattice pie crust. If you are not adding a lattice crust and instead are adding the top crust in one piece, use a sharp knife to cut a few slits in the top of the crust to allow steam to vent.
- Trim excess dough from the top crust or lattice strips, and then fold the overhang underneath itself, forming a thick rim. Press it together or crimp it with your fingers (or use a fork).

- Whisk the egg with a tablespoon of water, and then use as an egg wash by lightly brushing the top crust. This adds shine and helps the crust brown.

ASSEMBLE PIE

- Place the prepared pie onto a baking sheet lined with parchment paper (this can be the same lined baking sheet used for chilling the top crust). Bake the pie for about 75 minutes, turning a few times for even browning.
- If you notice that the pie crust is browning too quickly, mold a large piece of foil over a bowl that's been placed upside down to make a foil dome. Place the foil dome over the pie for the remaining bake time. This will slow the browning.
- Apple pie is done when the juices are bubbling through the vents of the top crust or lattice. If you do not see bubbles, the pie needs more time. Another way to check for doneness is to use an internal thermometer. Pierce the pie in the middle then test the temperature. The pie is done when it reads 195 degrees Fahrenheit (90C). Piercing the pie is also a nice indication of how soft the apples are. If they feel too crunchy, the pie needs more time.

BAKE PIE

- Be sure to cool the pie, without slicing into it, for at least 1 hour, preferably longer. Keep in mind that the pie filling does not fully thicken until it is completely cooled. So, for the absolute best results, cool the pie to room temperature, and then place it into the refrigerator for an hour or two.
- Waiting to cut into the pie until cool will prevent a soggy slice.

CHAPTER TWENTY-TWO

CARAMEL CUSTARD

INGREDIENTS

- 1/2cup sugar
- 3eggs, slightly beaten
- 1/3cup sugar
- 1teaspoon vanilla
- 1/8teaspoon salt
- 2 1/2cups very warm milk
- Ground nutmeg

INSTRUCTION

- Heat oven to 350°F.
- Heat 1/2 cup sugar in heavy 1-quart saucepan over low heat, stirring constantly, until sugar is melted and golden brown. Divide sugar syrup among six 6-ounce custard cups; tilt cups to coat bottoms. Allow syrup to harden in cups about 10 minutes.
- Mix eggs, 1/3 cup sugar, the vanilla and salt in medium bowl. Gradually stir in milk. Pour over syrup in cups. Sprinkle with nutmeg.
- Place cups in rectangular pan, 13x9x2 inches, on oven rack. Pour very hot water into pan to within 1/2 inch of tops of cups.
- Bake about 45 minutes or until knife inserted halfway between center and edge comes out clean. Remove cups from water. Cool 30 minutes. Cover and refrigerate until serving or up to 48 hours.
- To unmold, carefully loosen side of custard with knife or small spatula. Place dessert dish or plate on top of cup and, holding tightly, turn dish and cup upside down. Shake cup gently to loosen custard. Caramel syrup

will run down sides of custard, forming a sauce

CHAPTER TWENTY-THREE

CHOCOLATE MOUSSE

INGREDIENTS

- 1 cup heavy cream(240 mL)
- 3 tablespoons sugar
- 2 oz chocolate(60 g), milk or dark, broken into small pieces
- ¼ cup heavy cream(60 mL), hot
- 6 raspberries, to garnish
- 2 sprigs mint, to garnish
- 2 tubes tube cookie, to garnish

INSTRUCTION

- In a large bowl, combine the heavy cream and the sugar, beating with an electric mixer until soft peaks form when lifted from the bowl. Set aside two large spoonfuls of the whipped cream to garnish with at the end.
- Whisk the chocolate and hot cream in a separate bowl until smooth, then fold in the mixture into the cream with a spatula until no streaks remain.
- Split the chocolate cream mixture evenly between two martini glasses or your serving dish of choice, then chill for at least 1 hour.
- Garnish with a spoonful of whipped cream, raspberries, mint, and the chocolate cookie.

CHAPTER TWENTY-FOUR

FRUIT TART

INGREDIENTS

For the pastry cream:

- 2 cups whole milk
- 1 cup granulated sugar
- 6 egg yolks
- 1/4 cup cornstarch
- 1/4 teaspoon Salt
- 1 teaspoon vanilla extract

For the tart dough:

- 7 tablespoons butter softened
- 1/2 cup powdered sugar
- 1 egg
- 1/2 teaspoon vanilla extract
- 1/4 teaspoon Salt
- 1 1/4 cups all-purpose flour sifted
- 1/4 teaspoon baking powder

For the fruit tart:

- 1 pint Fresh cut fruit such as strawberries, blueberries, blackberries, raspberries, peaches, mango, and kiwi
- Apricot jam melted, as needed

INSTRUCTION

To make the pastry cream:

- In a medium non-aluminum saucepan over medium heat, heat milk until tiny bubbles appear on the surface, about 6 to 8 minutes (180 degrees). Stir to prevent scalding.
- In a large bowl, whisk together egg yolks and sugar. Whisk in cornstarch and salt. While whisking constantly, pour in half of the hot milk. Whisk in remaining hot milk and return to saucepan.
- Cook over medium heat, whisking constantly, until the mixture thickens to a firm consistency, about 5 to 8 minutes. Whisk in vanilla and pour in to a bowl.
- Cover with plastic wrap, pressing it directly on to the surface of the pastry cream. Refrigerate until chilled, about 2 to 3 hours.

To make the tart dough:

- In a standing mixer fit with the paddle attachment, or with an electric mixer by hand, cream the butter and sugar together on medium-high speed until pale and fluffy, about 3 minutes.
- Scrape down the sides of the bowl and add egg. Continue mixing until combined, scraping down the bowl as necessary. Add vanilla and salt and mix until combined.
- Reduce mixer speed to low. Add flour and baking powder and blend until the dough comes together (do not over-mix). Scrape dough onto a piece of plastic wrap. Wrap tightly and chill at least 1 hour.

To blind-bake the tart crust:

- Preheat oven to 350 degrees. On a lightly floured surface, roll out dough to a thickness of 1/8-inch to 1/4-inch. If the dough crumbles or breaks apart, press it back together with your fingertips.
- Loosely roll the dough around the rolling pin, then gently unroll it over the tart, preferably with a removable bottom (9 inches, or substitute a pie plate).
- Press the dough firmly into the bottom of the pan and up the sides. Trim any excess dough. Cover the dough with parchment paper or foil. Fill with pie weights or dried beans . Bake 12 minutes.

- Remove pie weights or beans and parchment paper or foil. Return to oven and bake until golden brown and fully cooked, about 10 to 15 minutes longer. Cool completely.

To assemble the fruit tart:

- Fill cooled tart crust with chilled pastry cream. Arrange fruit in a decorative pattern.
- Using a pastry brush, brush fruit with melted apricot glaze (reheat as necessary if glaze cools and becomes too sticky).

CHAPTER TWENTY-FIVE

CHOCOLATE TRUFFLE CAKE

INGREDIENTS

- 500 gm cooking chocolate
- 1 cup butter
- 1 teaspoon vanilla extract
- 1 1/2 teaspoon baking soda
- 1/2 cup unsweetened cocoa powder
- 1 cup whipping cream
- 1 1/2 cup milk
- 4 eggs- brown
- 2 cup sugar
- 2 cup all purpose flour
- 1/2 cup caster sugar

INSTRUCTION
STEP 1

- Take a saucepan and add chopped cooking chocolate and 1/2 cup butter and cook it over low heat until both these ingredients melt and form a smooth paste. Remove from heat and keep aside for 10 minutes. Meanwhile, butter up your cake tin and preheat the oven to 180 degrees Celcius for 5 minutes. Remember: If you have more than one tins, you can grease all of them to make a layered cake, otherwise, you can also bake one cake and then cut it into layers.

Step 2 Combine the wet and dry ingredients

- Take another large bowl and add eggs along with sugar and vanilla extract to it. Beat it until smooth and then add in the chocolate mixture. Beat it again until smooth. In a different bowl, combine the dry ingredients such as flour, sugar and baking soda. Mix them well and add to the chocolate mixture. Mix it with light strokes and combine everything well.

Step 3 Put the cake to bake and prepare the filling

- Add this batter to all the cake tins or the single cake tin and bake for 30 minutes. To prepare the filling, take a saucepan and add the rest of the cooking chocolate with butter. Add in the caster sugar and whipping cream and form a smooth mixture. For the chocolate ganache, heat the cream over medium flame and just when it is about to come to a boil, add it to cooking chocolate in a bowl and whisk rapidly until a smooth, luscious cream is formed.

Step 4 Layer, decorate and serve!

- Now that the cakes have cooled, take them out and let them cool on cooling racks for about 10 minutes. If you have baked a single cake, keep a plate over the cake top and carefully slide a serrated knife through the cake, cutting an even-surfaced layer. Add the filling to each layer and top the top layer with ganache. Cover the cake properly with ganache. Follow the same steps for layering if you have baked more than one cake. Grate some more cooking chocolate on the top and serve!

CHAPTER TWENTY-SIX

TIRAMISU CAKE

INGREDIENTS

For the Cake

- 1 3/4 cups cake flour 175g
- 3/4 cup milk room temperature
- 3 large egg whites room temperature
- 2 tsp almond extract
- 1 tsp vanilla extract
- 1 cup granulated sugar
- 1 1/4 tsp baking powder
- 1/2 tsp table salt
- 3/4 cup unsalted butter softened but still cool
- 1/4 cup sour cream

For the Swiss Meringue Buttercream:

- 5 egg whites room temperature
- 1 ½ cup granulated sugar
- 1 pinch sea salt
- 2 cups unsalted butter room temperature
- 1 tsp vanilla extract
- 1 tbsp instant espresso
- 3 tbsp brandy

For the Syrup:

- 1 cup strong coffee

- 1/3 cup brandy
- 2 tbsp coffee liqueur
- For the Filling:
- 4 egg yolks large
- 2/3 cup sugar
- 1/2 cup whole milk
- 16 ounces mascarpone cheese at room temperature

For the Assembly:

- 1/4 cup cocoa powder unsweet
- 12 chocolate covered espresso beans

INSTRUCTION
For the Cake:

- Preheat oven to 350 degrees. Prepare two 6-inch cake pans. When finished, cakes will be cut horizontally making 4 layers.
- In a large bowl, mix the milk, sour cream, egg whites, and extracts then set aside.
- Sift the flour, sugar, baking powder, and salt into the bowl of a stand mixer. Mix at a slow speed. Add roughly tablespoon-sized pieces of room temperature butter to the flour mixture and mix on medium-low for an additional 2 minutes. You should end up with a relatively fine meal.
- Drizzle about half of the milk mixture into the mixer, while running on low. Scrape the bowl down then mix in the rest of the milk mixture.
- Distribute the batter evenly between the two pans.
- Bake for 27-30 minutes at 350F or until a toothpick inserted comes out clean.
- Invert the cakes onto a wire rack to cool completely.

For the Filling:

- Whisk the yolks and sugar in a heatproof bowl then place over a pot of simmering water making sure that the water does not touch the bowl.
- Whisk in the milk slowly.
- Whisk constantly until the combined ingredients have thicker consistency. The internal temperature of the mixture should register at

170 degrees when you finish.

- Remove bowl from saucepan. Set bowl in ice water. Whisk the mixture until it has cooled (around 1 minute).
- Place mascarpone cheese in a large bowl. Fold the mixture into the cheese, using a rubber spatula.
- Miix until it is ALMOST COMBINED completely. Word of caution: do not over mix or it can have a grainy consistency.

For the Swiss Meringue Buttercream:

- Add egg whites, sugar and salt in a bowl.
- Give the mixture a brief whisk.
- Place the bowl over a pan of simmering water. Make sure the water does not touch the bowl.
- Whisk the egg whites occasionally while it warms up. When the mixture has warmed, whisk it constantly. You will heat the mixture until it reaches an internal temperature of 160 degrees.
- Transfer the bowl to a stand mixer with a paddle attachment.
- While the mixture is running on low, add tablespoon sized dollops of room temperature butter making sure to let the butter incorporate before you add the next piece. In a small bowl mix 1 tbsp Instant espresso and 3 tbsp of Brandy then mix into the buttercream.
- You can transfer it to a piping bag or to a ziplock bag to store in the freezer for later. (When you're ready to use it, take it out of the freezer, bring to room temperature, transfer to a bowl and beat it for about 10 second to bring back the consistency).

For the Syrup:

- Mix the coffee, brandy, and liqueur. Set to the side.

For the Assembly:

- Cut cake layers in half
- Transfer cooled, mascarpone custard to a piping bag.
- Place first layer — cut side up — on a cake stand. Drizzle the coffee mixture on top (about 1/3 cup per layer).
- Pipe the mascarpone filling on top and dust with cocoa powder.

- Place next layer on top. Repeat until all layers have been added.
- Cover the cake in the Swiss Meringue and smooth. You can scrape the side for a "naked" look but that buttercream is so delicious you'll probably want a nice thick layer!
- Dust top with cocoa powder. Use the end of a spoon to remove to remove a ring of cocoa powder from the edge of the cake's top (this will allow your dollops to adhere).
- Pipe dollops of Swiss Buttercream in a ring formation around the top, using an 869 Tip. Any Star tip will do though.

CHAPTER TWENTY-SEVEN

JELLO DESSERT

INGREDIENTS

- 2 cups crushed pretzels
- ¾ cup melted butter
- 2 tablespoons sugar

Filling:

- 8 ounces of cream cheese
- 1 cup of sugar
- 1 cartoon frozen whipped topping, thawed

Topping:

- 3 ounces each of strawberry gelatin
- 2 cups boiling water
- 1/2 cup cold water

INSTRUCTION

- Mix the pretzels, butter and sugar in a large bowl.
- Put the dough in an ungreased baking pan, and bake for 10 minutes at 350 degrees.
- After it is cool, beat cream cheese with sugar until smooth. Stir in the whipped topping and spread over the pretzel crust.
- Once you are done, refrigerate until cool. The topping can be made in a small bowl. Dissolve the gelatin in boiling water, add cool water and chill

partially.
- Pour over the filling with care and refrigerate the dessert for 4-5 hours.
- Serve it

CHAPTER TWENTY-EIGHT

STRAWBERRY SHORTCAKE

INGREDIENTS

- Fruit layer and topping:
- 8 cups strawberries
- 6 Tbsp sugar
- 2 cups whipped cream

Shortcakes

- 2 cups white flour
- 5 tbsp sugar
- 1 tbsp baking powder
- ½ tsp salt
- 8 tbsp unsalted butter
- 1 egg beaten
- ½ cup whole milk
- 1 egg white

INSTRUCTION

- Crush 3 cups of strawberries in a bowl until they resemble a puree, while slicing the remainder of the strawberries and mixing them all up with the sugar.
- Let them macerate for a while. Preheat your oven. Combine the flour with 3 tbsp of sugar, the baking powder and the salt and mix together.

Mix the butter in with the flour, then add the beaten egg and the milk.

- Combine all the ingredients, then prepare a dough (making sure not to overwork it) and cut 6 round dough biscuits.
- Place them on parchment paper and brush them with beaten egg whites.
- Sprinkle the remaining sugar over them and bake until brown. Prepare the whipped cream, then assemble your shortcakes by cutting your cooked biscuits into halves, then adding a portion of the sugar strawberries and whipped cream in between the two halves.
- Decorate with strawberries if desired and you're done.

CHAPTER TWENTY-NINE

CARAMEL CRUNCH ICE-CREAM

INGREDIENTS

- 1 litre low-fat vanila caramel swirl ice-cream
- 125gr chopped butternut snap biscuits
- half a teaspoon of ground cinnamon
- chopped dry roasted pecans
- wafle cones for serving

INSTRUCTION

- Put the ice-cream in a bowl to soften up.
- Once it is soft enough, add the biscuit crumbs, cinamon and pecans.
- Place back in the ice-cream container and freeze for a few hours.
- Serve in scoops and add some syrup if you like.

CHAPTER THIRTY

FRUIT AND ALMOND TART

INGREDIENTS

- 1 ½ cups of Multi-Grain crackers, crushed
- ¼ cup granulated sugar
- 1 teaspoon of cinnamon
- ¼ cups of butter, melted
- 12 ounces reduced-fat cream cheese, softened
- 1/3 cups of firmly packed brown sugar-flour
- ¼ cups milk
- ¼ teaspoon almond extract
- ½ cup finely chopped almonds (toasted)
- 3 cups of strawberries, seedless grapes, raspberries, blueberries, bananas, oranges etc.
- ¼ cup red currant jelly, melted

INSTRUCTION

- In a bowl, mix the multi-grain crackers, granulated sugar and cinnamon. Next you have to add the butter and mix until combine.
- Add the dough to a 9 ½ – 10 inch tart pan with a removable button and bake for 8-10 minutes at 350-400 degrees Fahrenheit. Cool completely.
- Separately, beat cream cheese with brown sugar, milk and almond extract until fluffy.
- Add the almonds. This mixture will be put on top of the cooled dough. The last step is to top with fruit and drizzle jelly.

- Put in the freezer for one hour, and serve.